Four Weeks: Reflections for Advent

Jeffrey Nelson

Published by Pine Candle Books, 2023.

FOUR WEEKS: REFLECTIONS FOR ADVENT

First edition. October 2, 2023.

Copyright © 2023 Jeffrey Nelson.

ISBN: 979-8223096771

Written by Jeffrey Nelson.

Table of Contents

Preface

For many years, I found it difficult to become excited about Christmas.

I would greet the decorations in mid-autumn with a certain disdain, groaning at their imposition into my favorite season. They would be my first reminder that I was in for another year of memories of years' past when certain loved ones were still around. They would also remind me that it was almost time for ministry activities that had aided in turning what used to be a treasured time into a slog of obligations in my role as a local church pastor.

I have only recently begun to process that latter point. I didn't realize how much my ministerial responsibilities in the month of December had an effect on my heart's slide into melancholy when garlands and lights began to appear and carols began playing in stores. There were other factors, of course, but this was one unexamined for most of the time that I undertook the planning of special worship services and other events. Had I been honest with myself and others sooner, perhaps it could have been salvaged.

I am happy to report that things have improved the past few years as I have undertaken a different path in my vocational life, one that does not bring such obligations during the last month of the year, other than a felt need to give plenty of support to those still needing to oversee these special events. I was, I must be quick to say, generously taken care of and shown appreciation by my congregations around Christmastime. These gestures were crucial to my ability to wake up Christmas morning and greet the day with the joy that eluded me for most of the month prior.

Many people experience Christmas in this similar manner. It usually is not due to pastoral responsibilities, but there may nevertheless be responsibilities to family that must be tended. And so for that reason, this sense of stress is quite widespread. For many others, it may be the reminder of who will not be celebrating with us this year due to death or distance. For still others, this holiday amplifies feelings of loneliness, sadness, anxiety, or grief.

But that's also why we have Advent. Far from being just a month-long prelude to Christmas, it is a time to acknowledge our deepest needs as we anticipate new birth. This is the season for those despairing, in need of hope, feeling abandoned, struggling with loss. It's a season for us to name what is keeping us from becoming caught up in the celebration in which everyone around us already seems to be partaking.

Advent is when we name what's weighing us down, in the hope that Christmas will lift us up.

The reflections that follow were written over a period of many years. Most of them were written while I was a pastor. My struggle in ministry related to this season will be quite apparent. But you will also see the signs of reassurance that I was able to find along the way. My hope is that reading about mine might help you find your own.

This book is divided into a week's worth of entries for each week of Advent. Each week also follows the traditional themes of the four candles around the Advent wreath: hope, peace, joy, and love. I set it up so that, if you choose, you can use it like a traditional devotional, reading one entry per day. You are also free to read it at a different pace if you like. There is also an entry each for Christmas Eve and Christmas Day.

However you use this book, I pray that you find what you are looking for this Advent season. I hope that you are able to be honest with what you need most, and that the arrival of Christmas provides an opening for you to find it. And I hope that in some small way, this book will help you do that.

First Week of Advent

First Sunday of Advent: Greens

Near the beginning of Advent, my hometown church always had a Hanging of the Greens service. This was a special service during which the decoration of the sanctuary for the season would be woven into the liturgy, with each piece of garland and every strand of holly and ivy accompanied by a reading explaining what they symbolized, followed by a few verses of a song as it was hung somewhere around the room.

I generally remember it as a meaningful time; a fine introduction to this special time of year that I in my junior high through college years could appreciate.

The church in which I served my third year of seminary had this type of a service as well. What I remember most from this was not the songs or the scriptures or the descriptions, but the organization and the stress.

This was a larger church in an affluent suburb of St. Louis, where things happened on time and with great efficiency. In the lead-in to this service, people needed to be assigned decorations to be paraded in and readings to give. They needed to be lined up in just the right way outside the sanctuary alongside a series of rectangular tables with every wreath numbered and labeled. And they needed to walk in at just the right time, go to just the right place, and hang them in just the right way.

This service was a great source of anxiety for the ministry staff. Whether they put it on themselves or whether members of the congregation impressed it upon them, there was an expectation that Hanging of the Greens needed to be The Perfect Beginning of the holidays. Things running smoothly during this service would bring tidings of comfort and joy to those who attended, which is what some not only expect but even demand from this time of year.

For as long as I was in full-time ministry, I consider myself fortunate that I never had to organize such a service. The two churches I pastored preferred to have volunteers showing up the day before Advent began in sweatshirts and jeans to pull down boxes from high places and hang things at a leisurely, less demanding pace. There were sometimes arguments about how best to space the ornaments on the tree and there was sometimes some confusion as to where certain things went, but we could figure that out without the eyes of the congregation upon us and without even our own inner voices willing us to feel happy or reverent as we fumble to arrange the nativity set on the altar just so.

People come to this season with a lot of different expectations. We may expect to adhere to certain traditions or sing certain songs or feel certain feelings. These activities are what help make this time what it is for us. And depending on how high those expectations are, our holiday experience is always under threat of ruination if things don't happen in just the right way.

I admit that I have some of those expectations for myself, although they've been tempered by various things over the years, enough that I can hold them loosely enough while adhering more closely to hope. I can hope in the underlying spirit of carols and get-togethers and silly movies and Linus's speech and the looks on my children's faces as our own decorations go up without fanfare.

I can hope that this season will bring comfort and joy, less from having things go precisely the way I want, and more in the midst of—and sometimes despite—the imperfection of what actually happens.

First Monday of Advent: Blueberries

My grandmother used to make muffins from scratch. She made a lot of things this way; she wasn't much for processed or frozen food. But for whatever reason, I especially remember the muffins.

Her way with ingredients was to use real stuff with every step: butter instead of margarine, actual eggs instead of that yellow stuff that comes in a milk carton. In her kitchen you weren't going to score much that was low-fat or that had the words "substitute for..." on the package.

You come to Grandma Nelson's house, you better come expecting to gain some padding for the winter. Hashtag sorry not sorry.

Blueberry seemed to be a favorite of hers. To be honest, I don't remember her making other kinds of muffins very often, if at all. The pans she used had cup sizes that allowed you to eat one or two in a few bites, and the berries themselves tended to sink to the bottom of the mixture as they baked, so once you got to those last few mouthfuls your taste buds were awash in buttery blue heaven.

Grandma had a love of cooking, and she cooked because she loved. Food was one of her ways of expressing affection to family and friends. Whenever she insisted that we grab another helping, we tended to chalk it up to her being a child of the Depression where sustenance was much more precious and harder to come by. But I look back and can see the ways she used food to show people how much she cared.

This was no clearer to me than on days when she made muffins. They tended to be a random afternoon treat, sometimes right after lunch and sometimes later in the day. But when she set to baking, we knew not to wander too far lest we miss them fresh out of the oven. We ate them huddled around her kitchen table while catching a squirrel hopping through the yard out the window and daytime TV buzzing behind us on her little black and white screen.

I still enjoy blueberry muffins, but there's always something missing from them. The ones I order at coffeehouses or get at the store lack the taste and the soul that those days brought, though I suspect that it's because I'm judging them by everything that those days were, far beyond muffins alone.

We've entered a season that amplifies these blueberry memories for me. This is a month that assures us that store-bought happiness is enough. Yes, those homemade things are nice, but the real joy lies in box stores and online deals. Entrust your holiday to us, and we'll get you through.

Occasionally, some genuine taste of times long past comes back, though never through what commerce promises. Through muffins or song or watching my kids' excitement, I feel what I felt before and I am thankful.

This time of year, my hope is not in what I can will myself to feel or what artificial substitutes for my memories I can find to get through to January. My hope lies in those small ways that something real ends up poking through. I don't have to look for it or force it into existence.

It just eventually arrives, whether I'm prepared for it or not.

First Tuesday of Advent: Belt

In October of 2021, I earned my red belt in karate. The belt tests in my dojo's system become longer each time due to the increase in techniques that you have learned since the last one, plus the fact that you have to review a fair amount from previous tests along with the newest material.

As a result, this test took nearly three hours. It was a marathon of an evening that demanded everything I could give mentally and physically, and then even more on top of that. I frequently wondered how I'd be able to keep going, thinking I'd already spent what I had, only to find that I still had a little more left.

Not only are these tests of technique, they are also tests of endurance. In fact, the black belts who oversee these might say they're actually more a test of the latter than the former: how much can you put up with before you reach the end of yourself, and are you able to go beyond that?

You may be able to imagine that one who anticipates these can't just sit around in between. If you're not doing a certain amount of exercise and preparation on your own time in addition to attending classes, you're likely to find that end of yourself more quickly. My awareness of that fact was one of the reasons I chose Practice as my One Word for 2021: this was one of the things to which I'd need to devote considerable practice time in order to complete successfully.

On the other hand, there's this quote from Winston Churchill that I recently discovered: "Plans are of little importance, but planning is essential." A specific step-by-step plan—whether for a belt test or a work project or something to do with family—has a lot of potential to go wrong. However, preparation and practice are nevertheless critical to adjusting to when that happens. It's the more elegant version of Mike Tyson's similar quote: "Everybody has a plan until they get punched in the mouth." Have you prepared for when that happens so that you can change your approach on the fly?

Advent is about nothing if not preparation. The encouragement to prepare for what's coming is all over our hymns and carols, in our candle liturgies, in the lectionary scriptures, and in devotionals. Prepare ye the way of the Lord, and when you think you've done enough preparing, keep going because we're still not there yet.

But we need to talk more about endurance this time of year as well. The early texts we get during this season aren't full of Hallmark sentiments. These stories don't have the big city executive returning to their quaint flannelized hometown for a happy ending with their high school sweetheart. Instead, they're about people tested by despair, poverty, oppression. They're being pushed to the end of themselves, and they're in search of hope.

2000 years later, as a pandemic has claimed over 6 million lives worldwide and continues to disrupt whatever we used to call "normal," as non-white people continue to cry out for their stories and experiences to be taken seriously, as those strained financially continue to reach for any crumbs they can receive from powers and principalities unbothered with slow-rolling any form of relief, how can we not keep talking about endurance?

The reality of the chaos around us is enough to throw a wrench into any of our perfect holiday plans. That's when our Advent planning and preparation takes over, and we discover what real hope entails.

First Wednesday of Advent: Crumbs

During my decade and a half as a pastor, I developed a certain relationship with the month of December. I won't deign to pinpoint when it started exactly, because I don't think that it can be measured that precisely. It's been more of a gradation; a slow setting upon over time that, when fully realized, can bring surprise that anything had ever changed at all.

Many people rely on the magic of this time of year to carry them, even to renew them. All the music and traditions bring a transcendent, spirit-brightening feeling that may float them through the month and into the new year, and then the anticipation slowly builds over the next 11 months until it may begin again.

For me, the magic went in the opposite direction. There was no single cause. Some of it was the death of loved ones that caused annual holiday trips to fade away. Some of it was the weight of needing to create magical moments for other people via my vocation to the point that there would be none left over for me.

And so, come mid-October when the decorations and ads began their annual early overtaking of anything related to autumn, I would groan inwardly at the impending weight re-asserting itself, with crumbs of magic falling from the table I was charged with setting so that I could collect them and save them up for when I could enjoy them the most.

This would be my inward reaction every year, without fail, for the better part of 15 years.

And then my first year after stepping out of the pastoral role, I wandered into a store to pick up some items. It was the later part of October, so I already knew what I would see: rows and shelves lined with all manner of knick-knacks and wall hangings proclaiming the merriment of the celebration to come.

This time, however, an inward shift had occurred. I did not greet this sight with the usual despair or resignation or anger or annoyance.

Instead, I felt a certain indifference, and even anticipation at what the appearance of these items signaled.

So much of December 2020 and beyond has not been what anyone has wanted. For my own part, I've lost vacations and work trips, I've had to readjust my expectations for settling into and performing my new position, and I've had to figure out how to balance work and family in a new way. I have little doubt that I have been alone in this recalibration of...basically everything, really.

There is a good chance that many people who already anticipate this time of year are leaning into it even more heavily than before. So much else has been upended, but the magic of this season has not abated. Instead, people need it in even greater abundance.

I not only noticed the shift within myself, but embraced it. If the shackles of some previous way of relating to this season have finally fallen away, then I would receive the new freedom that would replace it with gratitude.

I would receive hope, which had been there before, yet now seems to come as a full meal rather than crumbs, at long last.

First Thursday of Advent: Weeds

Our previous home was in an allotment of McMansions marked by small trees dotting streets every few feet and well-manicured lawns regularly cut and watered.

This neighborhood looked the way it did because our Homeowners Association dictated that individual owners adhere to a certain level of standards and practices. We knew what we were in for when sitting down with the builder to design our house, because at that stage we were told things like what colors for siding and shutters we couldn't choose on account of the houses in our immediate vicinity already having them. Even with this early warning sign of what could later transpire, we agreed to the terms set to us.

We were on a corner lot, which meant a comparably larger area of land and sidewalk to maintain. Our lawn included several mulch beds: one that wrapped around the side of the house and two that rose like islands in our side yard. It looked good when first put in, and we took pride in what we'd accomplished through our entire endeavor toward first-time ownership.

Eventually, we both became busy with the general responsibilities of our careers and caring for a toddler, such that we began to neglect the care of our landscaping. I still mowed faithfully, but the weeds in our mulch began to assert themselves in unruly ways. We both knew that they looked really awful and were no doubt an eyesore to anyone who passed by.

After enough weeks gazing out at the jungle emerging around our trees and plants, we began taking steps to address the situation. It was a team effort: my wife would pull the weeds in a designated area, and I'd soon follow up by spreading bags of mulch. We worked slowly over many evenings and weekends, but the improvement was noticeable and nearly immediate.

With just one modest patch of overgrowth left, we received a letter from the firm managing our allotment stating that they'd received complaints from members of our neighborhood about the state of our yard. This both puzzled and angered us, because we were almost finished dealing with the problem. Whether there was a delay in this faceless entity an hour away getting to the issue or one of our neighbors choosing to ignore the progress that would have been obvious by that point, we couldn't say. Regardless, I composed a letter back saying that we were very aware of the issue and had, in fact, almost completed addressing it. We never heard back, and we didn't really care, and this incident was one of the many we'd stack on a pile of reasons why we were thankful eventually to move someplace else.

Ours is a culture that doesn't deal well with weeds. It demands a certain exterior in exchange for a sense of security and well-being. We try our best to live by this unspoken code: if I keep my imperfections hidden, and you yours, we will be able to coexist in relative peace and harmony under the pretention that all is well. But there come those times when we can't hide so easily; our problems become so overwhelming that we end up having to address them in public whether we want to or not. And a certain subset of people love to watch, to nitpick, to say we're going too slow, to report our blemishes to whomever will listen. If any of this aids in removing them from others' points of vision, all the better.

This time of year ratchets up this tendency tenfold. It's a season of comfort and joy, after all, where we tell ourselves and each other that if we hang enough tinsel and crank up Mannheim Steamroller, we won't have to see or hear our own shortcomings, let alone those of others. The social contract of December often demands that if we hide our problems behind the presents under the tree, we can get back to them after New Year's. Otherwise, a letter from Santa, baby Jesus, and the Ghosts of Christmas Past, Present, and Future will be forthcoming.

One would think that a season where we tell a story about a peasant family having to resort to tending a newborn among animals would feature more understanding and permission-giving, especially when the four weeks beforehand are supposed to be for acknowledging how much we need that baby to be born and for that light to shine. And if we listen more closely to that story and block out the commercials and the piped-in mall music, we may realize that actually, we do have such permission to be real about our struggles and hang-ups, and to admit that all the manufactured joy doesn't compare to the genuine article.

This first week of Advent is for hope. That hope doesn't always look like smiles draped with weed-free holly and ivy, but at least it's real. And real is what we're waiting for.

First Friday of Advent: Bubbles

I enter the coffeehouse as I do most Friday mornings. I've been coming here often enough that the barista knows I'll want a mug of whatever dark roast they're serving. I chuckle to myself every week when he starts my order before I do. I'd also like breakfast, and they have one of the most amazing omelets I can find in the area, so today I feel like having one of those.

I take my mug to my table and open my laptop. I soon discover that I've forgotten my flash drive so I won't be able to do the church-related stuff that I'd planned to take care of, so I click to my blog's content management system instead.

It's time to start writing another series of Advent reflections. I've been doing this for so long that, even if nobody else in the entire universe expects me to do these every year, I still expect it from myself. Unfortunately for me, however, this year the blinking cursor on the empty white screen seems to have taken on a slightly mocking tone.

If there's a way to blink in an adversarial manner, this cursor has found a way.

My gaze drops from the screen to my coffee. Some bubbles have congregated around the outer edges. I watch them float, adjusting themselves to the slight movement of the table.

A toddler, happily babbling to herself as her mom urges her toward the door, catches my attention and I smile. The mom offers a small smile back.

They pass. My eyes drift back to the screen. The cursor blinks.

I'm supposed to be thinking about hope this week. That's the traditional thing. Find some metaphor for hope, and write about it. Come on, the cursor says, you've done this how many times? You can find hope in things like weeds and blueberries, so let's do it again.

I admit that I'm a bit distracted this time around. I'm thinking more about impeachment hearings and children in cages at our border. I'm preoccupied with the flash drive I left at home and a workshop I need to lead tomorrow and a prescription I need to fill.

Is there hope in so much worry and conflict and responsibility? What is there to hope for in the midst of all of this? What does hope look like in so much uncertainty?

My head drops again and I watch the bubbles. They just keep floating, doing their best as the darkness moves around them.

And then, just like that, I finally have my answer.

First Saturday of Advent: Daydream

The mental image first appeared sometime in mid-October, I think. It could have been earlier, but that's when I really started paying attention.

I tend to recoil at the kitschy side of Christmas. The annual and predictable parade of cheese-tastic songs that every radio station churns out. The cheap plastic decorations and knick-knacks that litter store aisles. The inflatable yard monstrosities that have become popular in recent years.

I just can't stomach most of it. So many people try so hard to create something magical this time of year, but most of what we have to work with is offensive to the senses and to good taste.

So I was somewhat taken aback when I started dwelling on the following scene: a dimly-lit pub. Tinsel and lights half-heartedly strung along the back of the bar. A tree in the corner that perhaps could use a little straightening. And the company an interesting mix of the lonely and upbeat. It's a few days after Christmas so there's a slight lilt to the proceedings. A low-tier college football bowl game silently plays on TV while some of the aforementioned cheese-tastic songs play over the sound system.

This was somehow an inviting scene for me. I wanted to be there, to soak in the atmosphere, the decorations, the music, the underwhelming football game. I sat with this for weeks, turning the image over again and again, wanting yet not wanting it, and wondering why this was stuck in my head at all.

It was just as I was beginning one of my early morning workouts that I realized why I wished for this scene so badly: it's because I had actually been there.

It was just after New Year's in 2007. My wife and I, along with my brother and his wife-to-be, made a trip to New Jersey to see my grandparents. We watched the ill-fated Rose Bowl between Michigan and USC, spent a day in New York City, and enjoyed a visit with my father's sister and her family, part of which was spent in a pub still decorated for the season catching up with our cousins. An unspectacular bowl game was playing on the TVs.

I wanted this mental scene not out of some irrational, unprovoked longing. Instead, it was because I associate it with an actual holiday memory spent with loved ones. My grandma died that summer, so this was one of the last times I was able to spend time with her. I'd see my grandfather only a handful of times before his death two years later. As it turns out, that couple of days spent in New Jersey was more special to me than I'd ever realized before just a few months ago.

The first Sunday of Advent is always spent thinking about hope. I suppose that one of my hopes this year is for a moment that only exists in my memory but that I want to re-create. I can keep imagining, I suppose. But I can also make new memories with others I love. Then, in its own way, the hope of this little daydream could come true.

Second Week of Advent

Second Sunday of Advent: Dog

In the spring of 2018, against my preferences and despite my concerns, my family got a dog. She was still a puppy at that point, having been born in January. Couple that with her being a Chihuahua mix, and you can imagine the small bundle of never-ending energy that we added to our household.

It's not that I mind dogs. I'll gladly give attention and affection to those who are not my own. But to me the actual owning of one is like having another child: they seem to require so much constant vigilance. Not a day goes by when I'm not pulling a toy or a shoe out of our canine companion's mouth, or cleaning up wayward droppings that couldn't have waited for the yard.

When she wants to be, of course, she's very loving. She'll curl up to doze on your lap or chew on one of her own actual toys next to you on the couch. She greets everyone who walks in the door with excitement and is happy to get to know new and familiar faces, sometimes with her tongue.

Having a dog has changed so much about how we live our day to day lives. We're more mindful about how long any of us will be gone and she'll be alone. We're more intentional about placing important items on shelves, counters, or hooks out of the reach of her eager teeth. Bedtime routines now include having one of us stay downstairs with her while the other tucks in the kids, lest she bark and whine at the bottom of the stairs.

That first holiday season brought an additional set of tests for us as dog owners. I saw some of this coming months before we got there. Fortunately, we already knew certain necessary tricks from over a decade of owning cats, but a dog adds its own dimension.

The tree in general is always in danger. We've long known to place ornaments at a certain height, but this pine-needled addition is a constant object of curiosity for eyes, nose, and teeth. This is to say nothing of leaving wrapped presents where little claws and mouth have easy access. They had to be tucked away until occasions for opening them present themselves later in the month.

One of my own little joys about this time of year was spending moments of solitude near the tree, taking in its soft light and allowing myself some excitement about the growing pile of gifts for loved ones stored underneath.

The dog changed that. It's now something to be guarded, and some elements can't be set in their usual place. And as a result, the view has changed.

When your source of peace has been disrupted, how do you recover? We may not have to deal with a dog's effect on our decorations or not, but we may ask that question in other ways this time of year. For some, someone is no longer around to join in the celebration. For others, a living situation has changed. And maybe there are unexpected joys hidden in those changes that we haven't discovered yet. Maybe such disruptions only bring further uncertainty and peace will skip a year, to be uncovered sometime later.

I haven't yet found my own answer. But with my little chihuahua now settled on my legs, I'll study the tree's lights, waiting for it to reveal itself.

Second Monday of Advent: Tubas

I first tended to hear them around the middle of October.

My second church had a tuba group that used one of our classrooms as a practice space. Once a week or so, there would be a few extra cars in the parking lot, and I had a good hunch to whom they belonged. Even while walking up the sidewalk, my suspicion would be confirmed by the faint sound of low brass emanating from their designated room. I couldn't make out what they were playing from there, but once I stepped inside their chosen piece became clearer.

Most mornings I observed a routine of walking from my office to the kitchen where I find a coffeemaker ready to dispense caffeinated brown liquid into my waiting mug. My purposeful stroll always took me past the room where the tubas practiced, where I'd be serenaded to and from my intended destination.

In mid-October, their chosen selection was "It Came Upon the Midnight Clear."

Of course it was.

Our area boasts a large and well-attended Tuba Christmas event, but even besides that there surely would be other opportunities in the coming months to hear and play holiday favorites in the weeks leading up to Christmas. This was the time to practice and make ready for those future performances, because they were fast approaching.

In years past, I would have cringed at hearing such a tune so early. I like focusing on one special day at a time, and at that point my front porch was covered in pumpkins, skeletons, and light-up ghosts. I resist the "Christmas creep" as much as I can, in part because I want each holiday to truly be its own thing and in part because I have as much baggage with this late-December day as anyone else and don't feel like dealing with all that yet.

But on this fall day, I smiled. I opened my heart and let the carol inside, if for just a moment. Hearing it brought peace rather than agitation, for reasons I still can't name. On that morning at least, knowing that this celebration was coming caused comfort, and I would accept it wholly and without grudge.

I'll take peace where I can find it these days, even in Christmas music before Halloween.

Second Tuesday of Advent: Scent

When I began seminary, I bought a pine forest-scented candle for my apartment. That summer I had discovered how watching a burning flame had the power to quiet my soul and help center my attention on my own thoughts. Candles have aided thousands of people over the centuries in doing this, and with my studies just beginning I wanted to remind myself of what I was pursuing; that it wasn't just a degree but something deeper.

I often lit this candle late at night, during what I intended to be a time of renewal at the end of the day. Yet that first semester featured a much more difficult adjustment than I expected, so those evening sessions usually came with questions of identity and feelings of longing that often pushed me past a reasonable bedtime. The flame was my life raft in a sea of self-doubt, the scent an added bonus that I didn't intend.

This candle has made every move with me since. The wick has been burned far too low and drowned too often in wax for it ever to be lit again, but I can't bring myself to throw it out. I've always found a place for it on a bookshelf or desk or side table, and thankfully nobody yet has questioned its placement or thought disposing of it would be doing me a favor.

Even though I can't light it anymore, there's a power to this candle that largely goes unseen by the casual observer. Every so often I'll pick it up, put my nose right into the melted center, inhale, and be transported right back to my basement seminary apartment where it provided the flame by which I wrestled with God every night. A single whiff of this candle's particular aroma (no other "pine forest" scent has recreated it...believe me, I've investigated) brings it all rushing back, and I remember the One who held me in check and urged me forward in the dead of my own spirit's night.

Many people love this season because it means that you get to do certain things you don't do the rest of the year. It means baking snowman cookies with Grandma or singing carols in worship or going to that party that so-and-so always organizes. These events and activities make this time of year what it is.

But as much as Christmas can mean what you get to do, it can also symbolize the things you don't do any more. Maybe age or mortality has declared that we can't gather in Grandma's kitchen for baking any more. Maybe now "Silent Night" brings thoughts rushing back of someone no longer able to join in the chorus of voices. There's no party this year, because the host took a new job in another state and you don't talk as often as you used to.

It could be years since you stopped, but the right smell or song can bring the memories right back in a moment, and you remember what you used to do, and you've been wondering what this season is without them.

I smell my candle, and the difficulty of that time isn't really what overtakes me so much as how far I've come since. I needed those days of doubt and growth more than I knew as they happened. If this week is about peace, maybe thoughts of days gone by can bring it by reminding us of where we've been and who we've been with, but also who we've become by being there.

This peace becomes more complex as we get older. But beneath the smells and the sounds, it still wafts and flickers, calling us into quiet assurance.

Second Wednesday of Advent: Smile

It certainly wasn't the reaction I expected.

It was early November, not more than a day or two after Halloween. My daughter and I needed to run to Target, as is our tendency on my days off when it's just the two of us. We usually have a few small items to pick up, most likely because we've been assigned by my wife to get them. I don't mind, because it gets us out of the house for a little while, and my daughter is usually up for a ride, especially when it might involve Starbucks banana bread at the end.

I knew what I was going to see once we got there. With the late October holiday just passed, many stores fast forward to the end of December overnight. Costumes and rows of candy are quickly replaced by lights and fake evergreens. We can't waste any time, now can we?

Sure enough, back in the seasonal section, that corner of the store had undergone a fast transformation. What little was left from Halloween had been relegated to a lone clearance aisle, and merchandise for the commercial grandaddy of them all had already begun to overtake everything.

My daughter was amazed, still wondering after the few pumpkins that were remaining and not yet really paying attention to what was replacing it. At that point, she hadn't yet experienced a Christmas where she'd really been able to notice what's going on, although that changed once we decorated at home. Then she saw everything: the lights, the garland, the stockings, the tree. She's just as fascinated and in awe of it as I thought she'd be, her eyes twinkling as much as the small white bulbs that she won't leave alone. Her smile shines as bright. Brighter, even.

That day in the store, I didn't smile. In fact, I felt a bit of sadness for which I wasn't prepared. I still can't quite pinpoint its source. It could have been how quickly we as a culture shift from one celebration to the next, with no breathing room or down time. It could have been a certain melancholy about holidays past spent with family who are no longer around. It could have been a personal realization that I should start my own planning even if I'd rather wait until after Thanksgiving.

Whatever it was, it didn't let me greet this retail development with joy. And in fact, it made me wonder whether I would this year. There are certain years where I just never get into the spirit: I spend too much time thinking about its crass commercial aspects or the absence of loved ones to get into it much, and I thought that this might have signaled what my experience of the season would be this time around.

Fortunately, that has not been the case, at least too much. In fact, I'm glad to have been able to wrap myself into the parts of the season that bring me meaning, and for the most part block out the excess and noise. And in the times when that isn't enough, I have my children's excited smiles to sustain me.

Second Thursday of Advent: Change

The second year of my spiritual direction program featured a 50-hour practicum. This basically consists of meeting with people for at least 50 hours total for spiritual direction in whatever way you want to structure it, monthly meetings with a supervisor to go over a verbatim based on one such session, and some other reading and writing.

My practicum was pretty simple and straightforward: guide a pastoral colleague through the 19th Annotation version of the full Ignatian Spiritual Exercises, which will end up being 30-32 weekly meetings when it's all said and done, and offer the option of an abbreviated 8-week overview version of the Exercises to members of the church where I was pastor.

That fall, I met with three people for the 8-week retreats, so that was four people total with whom I met for direction so far that program year. No two retreats were the same, as no two spiritual journeys are the same.

One of the most notable takeaways for me was how more than one directee reported how much they've noticed their interactions with others changed. They reported times with difficult people where they were inspired to take a step back and prayerfully consider how to handle it rather than up the anxiety by snapping back. Their daily prayer time had seeped into other aspects of their lives. Here was the importance of spiritual health playing out for others to see.

Around that same time, my daughter was struggling with RSV. Her nose was incredibly stuffy, her chest congested. She'd be privy to coughing fits, even to the point of choking. Unfortunately, this choking has led to gastrointestinal pyrotechnics more than once, usually at the most inopportune times.

One such time occurred when we were already running late for a doctor's appointment. I'd just strapped her into her car seat when the coughing and subsequent vomiting happened. In the past when I've been in a situation like this, I've been privy to a complete freakout, albeit a brief one. This time, however, two things happened.

First, I remembered my directees reporting the difference in their spirits because of their prayer time when similar moments happened.

Second, a very clear voice in my head said, "You're no good to her when you're hyped up. She needs you to stay calm."

And so, letting go of how late we were, I set to work in cleaning her up and cradling her to calm her down. We would leave when we would leave. That was not the most important thing in that moment.

Whatever it is that my directees are learning from me, I'm learning just as much from them. At least indirectly, they helped get me through that morning. For that, I'm thankful. And during this week of the season when we're invited to reflect on peace, this will serve as the basis for my own reflection.

Second Friday of Advent: Tree

I slowly amble down the stairs, sleep still in my eyes, a hungry cat underfoot. My wife's alarm has woken me as usual. Rather than fight it, I've become accustomed to starting my day when she does. Actually, I start mine earlier: she'll hit the snooze button four or five times before actually getting up.

The timer on the coffeemaker is one of my best friends. Gone are the days when I'd fumble around sleepily with filters and grounds; I'm able to just pour myself a steaming cup. I savor that first sip, and fancy a second. Third. Okay, I can do other things now.

The newsletter from my hometown church sits on the kitchen counter not yet read. I pick it up along with a small devotional booklet that the instructor of my spiritual direction program gave to the class, and sit on the couch right next to the Christmas tree.

Aside from the modest ones under the kitchen cabinets, I haven't turned on any lights. The tree stays lit at all times. It's just something we do.

I take another few sips of coffee while lazily leafing through the newsletter. The pastor has written a fun reflection about how quickly we receive text messages and contrasts that with how slowly the message of Advent comes to us. Nice. There's an article requesting information about a plaque in the sanctuary honoring members who served and died during WWII. I know that plaque very well. There's news of the upcoming Christmas program and services on Christmas Eve. I think about attending the late service after my responsibilities at my own church are finished. I suspect I'll be too tired.

Finished with that, I start reading from the devotional. There's a poem in front, and then a series of prayers based on readings from Isaiah:

> The word that Isaiah son of Amoz saw concerning Judah and
> Jerusalem. In days to come the mountain of the Lord's house
> shall be established as the highest of the mountains, and shall

be raised above the hills; all the nations shall stream to it. Many peoples shall come and say, "Come, let us go up to the mountain of the Lord, to the house of the God of Jacob; that he may teach us his ways and that we may walk in his paths." For out of Zion shall go forth instruction, and the word of the Lord from Jerusalem. He shall judge between the nations, and shall arbitrate for many peoples; they shall beat their swords into plowshares, and their spears into pruning hooks; nation shall not lift up sword against nation, neither shall they learn war any more. O house of Jacob, come, let us walk in the light of the Lord! (Isaiah 2:1-5, NRSV)

I mull these words over for a few minutes, and then my mind wanders to other things: church, Christmas preparation, a recent conversation, how the year has gone.

This is the week when we're invited to think about peace. While the season, my transition, and certain other things don't always lend themselves to peace, I can at least enjoy these moments by the tree. May that peace somehow infuse itself in my entire day.

Second Saturday of Advent: Room

In our previous house, the first room immediately off to the right when you walked in the front door was our dining room. When we sat down to look at layouts and to plan to have our house built, the woman we were working with was slightly surprised that we wanted one; apparently, dining rooms are more rare in newer houses. It reflects another shift in the culture where more families are realizing that they just don't have many meals that necessitate such a room, so many opt not to set aside such a space. Instead, more and more families have more informal spaces off of the kitchen where most meals are shared.

And we're actually no different. We only ever had two meals in that room, both when we hosted family for Thanksgiving. Otherwise, that room didn't get a lot of use. But my wife had been given her grandmother's dining room set, and we needed someplace to put it, so we had a dining room.

Regardless of how often we used it for its stated purpose, it was a nice room. The furniture was in great shape. It had a nice big window with a view of the neighborhood. We always included it in our holiday decorating: an Advent wreath on the table, and a nativity scene on the sideboard. The longer we lived there, the more time I liked to spend in that room. In the early morning before the rest of the house is awake, I'd sit at the table with a cup of coffee just looking out the window, enjoying some quiet moments before it was time for *Phineas and Ferb*.

Even though I wasn't having a meal there, I used this room for its purpose: slowing down and just sitting for a while. Hosting a meal in a dining room implies too much time and effort and coordination and intentionality, and we're in a hurry. The dining room is quiet and slower, while all the busyness and noise took place in our morning room where most meals were actually consumed. So I like to think that I'm tapping in to the spirit of our dining room, and its invitation to just sit and exist and enjoy.

One morning, I caught myself thinking that once I got through the next week or so of activities at my church, I'd have more time to sit and enjoy this Advent season a little more. The logic is silly, and I should know better. This season is to be enjoyed in the midst of everything else, instead of spent hoping for some quiet moment that may never come. I'd sit in the dining room or wander the sanctuary or watch the snow out my office window knowing that I couldn't stay there forever; knowing that I have other responsibilities. But as long as I carry the peace of those spaces with me, integrating them with the rest of my life, then I won't have to wish away the days while missing this present moment.

Third Week of Advent

Third Sunday of Advent: Magnificat

"No politics in church," the church member, upset by something the pastor said during her sermon, says in the greeting line on the way out one Sunday.

The pastor could have said any number of things that brought this response, and she could have done so without mentioning any candidate or party.

She could have said something about racial injustice, or LGBTQ+ inclusion, or income inequality. She could have said something about violence against immigrants or women or transgender people. But this person heard it through their own political filters, formed by years of watching their favorite network or listening to their favorite pundits, and decided that this was out of bounds in the setting of a church.

(Never mind that "no politics in church" is usually only raised when someone doesn't like what they heard.)

The thing is, the Gospel is political. If it wasn't, then the powers that be in Jesus' day wouldn't have conspired to kill him (crucifixion was a political death). There are political messages all over the Bible, from the Mosaic law to the era of the kings to the prophets to Jesus' ministry to Revelation. God wants God's people to act a certain way in the world toward others, and to choose ways of living contrary to the empires of the day.

Advent is as political a season as any in the church. John the Baptist preached outside the city limits, riling up the religious leaders and calling out the king to the point of being thrown in prison and beheaded. Once Herod hears about Jesus from the Magi, he takes violent steps to try to protect his power.

And then there's Mary. Many are used to seeing her as this sweet little teenager looking longingly into the sky singing "Breath of Heaven." But she puts her life at risk repeatedly for her child, before and after he's born. And when she visits her relative Elizabeth and sings the Magnificat, it is anything but a nice little Amy Grant song:

And Mary said, "My soul magnifies the Lord, and my spirit rejoices in God my Savior, for he has looked with favor on the lowliness of his servant. Surely, from now on all generations will call me blessed; for the Mighty One has done great things for me, and holy is his name. His mercy is for those who fear him from generation to generation. He has shown strength with his arm; he has scattered the proud in the thoughts of their hearts. He has brought down the powerful from their thrones, and lifted up the lowly; he has filled the hungry with good things, and sent the rich away empty. He has helped his servant Israel, in remembrance of his mercy, according to the promise he made to our ancestors, to Abraham and to his descendants forever." (Luke 1:46-55, NRSV)

In her last book *Wholehearted Faith*, the late Rachel Held Evans has this to say about the Magnificat:

In the Magnificat, Mary isn't merely making a birth announcement. this prayer is definitely not the ancient Palestinian equivalent of a gender reveal party. Her words are not the scriptural equivalent of cutting a buttercream cake that turns out to have bright blue frosting inside. Instead, Mary's holy soliloquy seems breathtaking in its bravado: she declares the inauguration of a new kingdom, one that stands in stark contrast to every other regime—past, present, and future—that relies on violence and exploitation to achieve "greatness."

In some ancient liturgical volumes, the Magnificat was called by another name: the *Evangelium Mariae*, the Gospel of Mary. This seems right, because there is so much good news in her prayer. Mary proclaims that God has indeed chosen sides. And it's not with the powerful but with the humble. It's not with the rich but with the poor. It's not with the occupying force but with people who are occupied and oppressed, disregarded and disempowered. It's not with vain, narcissistic kings but with an unwed, unbeliever teenage girl entrusted with the holy task of birthing, nursing, and nurturing God.[1]

No politics in church? Even Mary can't abide that. Her famous song declares what side God is on, and who Jesus will open the doors of God's kingdom to. It's good news for those who need it the most.

God doesn't have a political party, but God does call people to speak and act on behalf of God's people, and that does have a political dimension. Mary's song helps provide the soundtrack.

[1]Evans, Rachel Held. *Wholehearted Faith*. New York: HarperOne, 2021, p. 143

Third Monday of Advent: Fields

The church my family attended while I was in elementary school was at the corner of several county roads, surrounded by barns and cornfields and little else.

What the area lacked in any kind of established neighborhood or easily accessible commerce, it made up for in space for a school-aged boy and his brother to play and indulge the imagination. We lived in the parsonage a few hundred yards up a hill that was perfect for sledding and a wide-open yard for all kinds of games.

This space always seemed to invite reflection for me in the weeks leading up to Christmas. The stories of shepherds in the fields took on a special meaning for me as I'd stand atop our hill, the snow falling around me, and I'd survey the fields surrounding us thinking of what it could have been like for them. Middle Eastern fields probably aren't much for corn, but the openness and silence told me something of what they could have known on a typical night before receiving their message from On High.

In the evening as the lights on distant radio towers began their slow blinking, I'd think of the star eventually making itself known to Magi, however many of them there actually were. These certainly weren't actual celestial bodies, but my younger self could pretend they were to make something of their journey come to life.

My first pastorate was a setting similar to these childhood years. We didn't have a good sledding hill, but we had a church and a parsonage on county roads surrounded by fields. We even had cellphone towers, one almost literally in our backyard, blinking away the night hours. It was a place that easily called back those earlier imaginings about shepherds and Magi trying to find their way, seeking signs of where they were meant to be going.

I always found a private joy in these imagined incarnations of the story. Those fields helped make it real to me. There was a certain loneliness that I felt in those years, where I was content to explore the tamed wilderness around my house. I knew something of passing the time in fields, and could relate to that part of the story. There was something of finding my way in open spaces that made sense to me.

My last two houses have been set in neighborhoods. You have to take a drive to find fields like what I used to know. But I still carry those fields within me, attempting to know where I am and where I'm going, especially when there's no easy indicator of what direction I'm meant to face.

The towers, however, are easier to come by; we have one that is visible from our house. It's a small, silly thing, but I can watch that faithful red light wink in the night, and still know that Someone beyond myself is leading the way.

Third Tuesday of Advent: Tires

I don't remember which year it was. I remember that my son was very young and we still lived in the house prior to the one we live in now.

By that point, our van had been in desperate need of new tires for months. The front ones were quite bald, but for reasons now lost to me—likely a combination of finances and scheduling—we hadn't yet made it a point to replace them.

I was home with my son for the day, so it was a Monday. We made our weekly trip to the town where my parents lived just for something to do. Grandma and grandson loved hanging out together, so I made it a part of our Monday mornings in those days. After our visit ended, we began the drive home, during which a snowstorm started to kick up, quickly covering the roads.

I thought we'd be fine before conditions became too bad. I was mistaken. We probably would have been okay had the semi truck in front of us not slowed to a stop on an uphill road, making it impossible for the van on its smooth tires to just pull around it and continue. Instead, I had to turn us around and find another route back to the house that involved less of an incline.

The next route I tried was on too much of a downhill slope. Despite having my foot on the brake, we slid right through a stop sign. Turning around would mean the same impossible climb upward.

At another intersection we were rear-ended. I was at a dead stop, so this wasn't the tires' fault. There was no damage, except to my increasingly fraying nerves.

The entire time, my son was watching *Sid the Science Kid* on the car's DVD player, quite oblivious to what was happening. To help ensure he was okay and to calm myself down, I kept asking him what Sid was learning about; what he and his friends were exploring together. I tried to feed off his innocent calm as much as I could, my concern for his safety welling up like a baseball in my throat.

The fourth attempt I made was successful. It featured a flat road, albeit still not yet plowed. The van was able even to get up the slight grade of our driveway and into the garage. The tight hug I gave my son once we were inside bewildered him; he just wanted to head to his toybox.

I point back to this experience as a turning point in my opinion of the winter season. For years after I would dread snow-covered roads, worried that I'd have to re-live this in some form. Although I am much more vigilant about how long either of our vehicles has been on the same tires.

It's been long enough now that I can see the more joyful aspects of this time of year again, but it has not come quickly or easily. Many are still unable to find joy in winter, let alone specifically the holidays, due to tragedies, traumas, or griefs perhaps years removed though still fresh.

I hope and pray for them, less for tidy resolutions and more for the tires they need to keep navigating through.

Third Wednesday of Advent: Pumpkin

I'm writing this near the end of September in a well-known chain that sells coffee and bagels. I was afforded some free time while a family member keeps an appointment, and so I ordered my own mug and pastry. Since it is still early in the fall months, I've ordered a pumpkin muffin, my first of the season. It tastes as delicious as I expect. I also could have chosen a pumpkin-shaped cookie with orange icing if I'd been so inclined, but today the muffin won out.

As I find an empty booth and begin unloading several items from my bag, my thoughts turn to what this place and most others will look like around the beginning of November. Pumpkin muffins will likely give way to ones with green or red sprinkles. The icing will change to those colors as well, the cookies themselves probably shaped like trees or ornaments. Tinsel will hang from the lights and carols will play softly over the speakers.

My first reaction to these thoughts is a silent sneer. I always lament Christmas' encroachment into my favorite season, where the autumn themes disappear too soon, at least from where I'm sitting. How early will it begin this year? How many pumpkin muffins should I hoard for later before they're taken away?

Then I begin to listen to the present moment. A man is on his phone wishing an unknown someone happy birthday, promising to buy them a present before he sees them next. Several students are on laptops clicking away on assignments. Two young women are engaged in a hushed yet passionate discussion about mutual acquaintances. Restaurant workers share information about orders they need to prepare. A little boy tells his father about his day. Each of them hold inside their own concerns, a little of which you can see or hear if you pay attention, but so much more is underneath.

I take a moment to wonder what they're worried about or what they're hoping for as soon as tomorrow. I wonder what's bringing them joy, since I'm writing this for the week when that's what we're especially supposed to be mindful of. I listen and look here for joy, and there is some, but it might be to mask something else or it might be even more elusive than that.

And when those tree cookies appear and that tinsel dangles above these same interactions, will joy be any more overt? And more importantly, will it be genuine? What are each of these people waiting for now that might come about by the time the decorations and songs and themed confections provide the backdrop for moments like ours?

How will joy arrive? How might it yet keep hidden?

For me, my joy is in this muffin. I'm trying not to look too far ahead because it means I'll miss the pumpkin-flavored now. Joy will manifest in another way by then. I'm content to wait and see.

Third Thursday of Advent: Lights

In my elementary school years, we lived in a parsonage out in the country, surrounded by corn and tarred gravel roads. Our nearest neighbors lived a half mile away, and other than the church there wasn't a whole lot of reason for the occasional car to stop or even slow down. We lived on the way to somewhere else.

Every December, we decorated like most other families. The tree was the main event, and we had a few other small items we'd hang or place in noticeable areas. Other than our artificial evergreen, my brother and I were probably most excited by the strands of colored lights that we used to outline the windows of the living room and our bedrooms. We had to take turns switching on the living room ones, but we were given complete autonomy with those in our rooms. We'd wait until it was just dark enough, and then either leave them on all night or unplug them again just before bed.

From the road, I can't imagine that these were much to look at. These smaller bulbs were perhaps barely visible from more than a hundred yards away. In addition, they constituted the extent of our outside decorations: we didn't put lights in trees or bushes or on the porch; we had no garland wrapped around banisters or railings. And nobody had yet produced the gaudy inflatable *Peanuts* characters that are now so popular. No, all we had were modest window lights, unimpressive to most, especially relative to the way some canvas their yard with all manner of holiday cheer.

But those lights excited us. And we didn't much care about the rest.

While driving after dark, I notice houses that are decorated like my childhood home. All they can muster are a few egg-sized bulbs around a window or a plastic Santa by the door. Maybe there's little more than a wreath at the entrance or a star on the chimney. They'll be passed unnoticed in favor of displays bigger and brighter; that people consider much more festive. People pass by what they see as half-hearted attempts on the way to somewhere else.

We'll never know the reasons why such houses do what seems like the bare minimum. Maybe that single strand is all they could afford, or they're too busy or fraught with anxiety to trouble themselves with much more. Maybe the season brings too many reminders of grief and loss, and even that plastic Santa is more than they wanted to do. Maybe that star on the chimney doesn't seem like much, but it's everything to the person who hung it, because they fought themselves to put it there at all.

This time of year, the smallest light is the best some can show.

Third Friday of Advent: Sanctuary

A colleague once posed the question on Facebook whether it was truly possible to preach four sermons about waiting with any sustained creativity and energy. I think it was asked in the context of expressing relief that one Sunday would feature her church's kids putting on a Christmas play in lieu of a sermon.

I could relate to that question, because I often asked it myself when I was a pastor. Some years, trying to find something new to say about Advent themes could be a challenge, especially since the overall theme of Advent boils down to waiting, preparing, waiting some more, having patience while we wait, hoping and waiting, waiting for peace, joyfully waiting, etc., etc., etc.

One Advent season while at my first church, my colleague's observation crept back into my consciousness during a different experience. It was late afternoon. The sun was already beginning to sink toward the horizon and darkness had begun to settle in. I'd finished my tasks for the day, had set my bag on the bench outside the office, and figured that I'd wander the sanctuary for a time before leaving.

This was one of those days when I was moved to remain silent as I walked. Maybe it was the dissipating light, maybe it was that I just wanted to be quiet after a day of interacting with others. At any rate, I was content to walk, to observe the decorations, to linger on and savor the time of year, to catch glimpses of the snow as I passed by windows.

As I walked, there seemed to be some other reason for my remaining silent. I still can't tell you what it was, but I have a better handle on it now than I did in the moment. I wandered, I lingered and savored, I reflected. I reflected on how the season has been going and how it always seems to pass so quickly. I reflected on how things are going around the church; how there seems to be an uptick in health issues, how various ministries are going. I reflected on my wife's impending graduation that next August and how that will give the family a little more breathing room in numerous ways. I reflected on Christmas shopping. I reflected on what I had to do the rest of the week and the rest of the season. I reflected on how relationships with church members had changed and deepened; the benefit of being around for six years.

Still, even in all that reflecting, there was something else. It wasn't exactly some sort of nagging feeling, it wasn't exactly a feeling that something has been left unfinished. The best way that I can describe it now is that it felt like I was waiting for something. I think I still am, but that afternoon I was especially aware of it. And it was a very present feeling, not an emptiness or something that I was trying to force. Rather, it was something both inside and outside myself, a gentle tension that made me take notice.

I eventually stopped by the pulpit and just watched, listened, and waited some more. I guess that I was hoping that whatever I was waiting for would make itself known. I sat there for at least ten minutes, wondering what exactly was stirring within or around me. It was as if I was hoping that something would burst forth from the silence, from the darkness, and reveal itself.

The light continued to fade, and I realized that I needed to get home. Whatever it was, whatever it is, I'm still waiting for it.

Third Saturday of Advent: Numb

I can recall very clearly what I was doing and how I felt on December 14, 2012.

I went to the church that and sat, pondering the immense amount of packing that I'd need to start before too much longer. I'd recently announced my call to another church, and there was much to do in the 3 months between that announcement and my departure. I went ahead and packed up some files that I knew I'd want to keep but wouldn't be needed in the next few months. That in itself was a moment that further communicated to me the finitude of this ministerial adventure I'd had for the past eight years.

Sometime that afternoon, I began reading about Newtown, Connecticut. The mentions of it on social media trickled at first, and then there was a deluge of conflicting news reports and raw reactions.

Senseless violence and death at an elementary school, many of the casualties a year or two older than my own son. This was far from the first mass shooting in 2012, but my reaction to this one was quick, surprising, and all-encompassing. You're not supposed to drop off your kindergartner at school, still full of innocent curiosity and playfulness, amazing and hilarious in the ways they verbalize connections between objects and concepts, and worry about them being gunned down without rhyme or reason, that innocence suddenly gone.

As more and more details began to emerge and more reactions began to register, it only took reading a four-word tweet to send me over the edge completely: "How long, O Lord?"

The benefits of serving a smaller church is that nobody is usually around to hear you openly weeping.

That night, the three of us went out to dinner while our house, already on the market, had a private showing. We decided on a popular pizza place I'd only ever experienced once in all the years we've lived in this area. It was a wonderful respite from the news, and the pizza was as good as it was the only other time I had it. But the family time was even better.

Unfortunately, the sadness returned on Saturday, which I spent agonizing over whether to change what I was going to preach, and if so, how. Maybe I could just get up and wing it, or maybe I could just tweak what I was going to say with some minor additions and references to the tragic events. Or maybe I could just speak for a few moments and just invite people to share their own stories of joy. I re-wrote portions, re-wrote the whole damn thing, went back to the original and just moved stuff around with little bits added in, and then just closed the laptop and gave up.

None of what I was coming up with was satisfying. Not a whole lot of anything was satisfying.

Nothing besides sitting on the couch with the family, sipping coffee and watching whatever bowl game happened to be on TV was satisfying. But seeking words to speak about joy of all things was not getting me anywhere.

I clearly didn't have a say in the matter, because Sunday morning eventually came. I got up early to practice what I had, and got halfway through before hearing my son stirring. I wasn't even going to be able to practice this poor excuse for a sermon, this wretched limp awful pile of crap that I'd have to give to a roomful of people because I had to say something (or so I assumed).

So I got up and started talking. I talked about how our culture tries to shove artificial joy down our throats this time of year and those of us who've known tragedy can see right through it. And I talked about Ignatius of Loyola's twin ideas of spiritual desolation and consolation, and how liberating and truly joyful it can be when the former gives way to the latter. And I talked about true joy being anchored in something, having a context and a reason. And I talked about why we even have a season like Advent leading up to Christmas; how we don't just rush into singing "Joy to the World" but instead reflect on our needs, or emptiness, our lack of joy, and how a song like "O Come O Come Emmanuel" is not just a reflective song but can also be a prayer, a crying out to God for liberation from whatever is keeping us captive.

And then I slumped into my chair, and we took the offering.

Did it speak to anyone? I don't know. Nobody really said one way or the other save for the usual "very nice"s that I get. Maybe I got myself way more worked up than others were. Maybe this sermon was more for me to begin with. And that's okay, too, I guess. Sometimes preachers preach to themselves just as much as they preach to others.

That night was our Blue Christmas service, which became one of my favorite services of the year in my time there. I noted a higher number of non-members that year. It seemed that many were seeking and finding something that this service offers.

I approached the tables of tea lights arranged along the front, and lit one for what was on my mind that season: my current church, my future church, the people of Newtown, my family, departed loved ones. This was yet another instance of worship ministering to me even as I led it.

I have plenty of reasons to rejoice, but also plenty that weighs me down. I was thankful for the glimmers of joy and of hope that I found throughout a very long, very tiring day. It was a day capped by wine and cake. And that's about as good an ending as one could hope for. My wife and I enjoyed it together, perhaps engaging in our own quiet rejoicing that the weekend had been managed as well as it could.

Fourth Week of Advent

Fourth Sunday of Advent: Nativity

Some changes are made with pre-planned purpose, and some...are not. The latter happens because someone doesn't know any better, or because it just makes sense to do it, or because one did things a certain way in a previous time and place and just assumed that it's done the same way where they are now.

My very first December at my second church, I arrived to help decorate the building for the upcoming seasons. I had no idea where anything was meant to go; no memory of what everything usually looks like. But it made sense for me to show up and do what I could.

We had several nativity sets that went up around the church. One is a fun mismatched set that looks like it was cobbled together from three or more sets.

The box containing these figures was placed in the sanctuary, so my natural assumption was that they went on the altar. My previous church had one there, so that must be where this one went, too. So I took it upon myself to set it up.

Several. Years. Later: I went about placing the nativity set on the altar, while another donated set was being set up on a table out in our narthex. I made some comment about how nice it was to have something on that table, to which someone responded, "Oh, usually the one from the altar goes there, but you changed that."

Again, not every change is pre-planned.

We could say that the change to the lives of Mary and Joseph in the announcement of Jesus' conception came with some planning and purpose. The various angelic visitors tip us off to that. The Holy Spirit meant to do what She did, and Jesus was going to have a divine calling to fulfill during the course of his life.

But in order to get there, Mary and Joseph were going to have to do some improvising. Having to hang out in a barn, much less coordinate a birth, was not planned. Having to make room for some shepherds with their own strange angelic encounter was not planned. The various trips in and out of Egypt in Matthew were fly-by-night sorts of moments.

As much as we may focus on the divine control of it all, the purpose behind Jesus' birth and all that he was destined to do, there was a lot to make up in the heat of the moment.

Even this late in the season, I don't have everything planned. Like many pastors tasked with worship leadership this week, there are a lot of moving parts to worry about, much of which depends on the volunteers around us. We give up control to involve others, which is necessary, because the celebration to come is not just ours alone. Not even when we accidentally change something.

But into that imperfection, Christ is born again. He'll change stuff, too. He'll do it while fully immersed in human experience and fully engaged with people's lives. He'll even change a few things by accident himself.

But even accidental changes make good stories. And good stories help us discover truths and possibilities that we wouldn't have considered without them.

So it's a good thing the story we tell this week is full of accidental changes. What will we discover through them this time?

Fourth Monday of Advent: Clouds

A certain day of the week, I wake up before dawn with a mission. I rise nearly every morning around the same time, but with this day comes an added responsibility that I undertake with the utmost seriousness. I stumble around in the quiet and dark to find my sweatshirt and footwear, grab my keys and wallet, and head off to pick up donuts for the family.

I have a 98% success rate getting out of the house before anyone else wakes up. That other 2% is thwarted by my daughter, who apparently inherited my morning-riser tendencies. What's more, she knows what I'm about to do and, for a time when she was in preschool, insisted that she ride along.

One morning where she caught me about to make my run, I secured her into her seat and we began our joint trek by the glow of the car's headlights.

"The clouds are so beautiful," the declaration came from the backseat, interrupting my pre-coffee reverie. I leaned forward to see the moon's light muted behind a misty curtain. I had to agree that the sight was charming, light peeking through before the sunrise. I heard how beautiful it was all the way to our destination, and all the way back, with breaks in between for a bite of chocolate donut before it resumed. Other than enjoying her special morning treat, it was the only view worth seeing and the only observation worth making.

This season comes with clouds. We search for light, but sometimes the fog is too thick to find it. Our grief or stress or fatigue billows into our eyes, and driving through all the traditions numb on autopilot is the best survival tactic.

When all seems lost, an angel appears unexpected and startling. Her voice pokes through just enough: look at the light. You might not always notice it, but it is for you and with you. And in that one moment when you can see it, even the clouds can become beautiful.

Fourth Tuesday of Advent: Houses

The caroling trip wasn't going the way I'd expected.

While at my second church, I'd helped organize its annual outing to visit our shut-ins and sing to them the songs of the season. The first few years I was there, we'd divide into two groups, each taking half the list. Given that we had so many, it seemed to be a sensible way to ensure that everyone was seen within a reasonable timeframe.

One year, several of my caroling families had other ideas, as they insisted that the entire group travel together to see everyone. That meant corralling 40 or so people to 10-12 different houses, the whereabouts of several of which I wasn't completely certain myself. My assumption had been that a group of around 20—3-4 carloads max—could navigate the unknown places with relative ease. Instead, we'd all engage in this adventure in guesswork together.

The evening proceeded without too much incident. While parking on several streets provided challenges and each household only got to hear maybe 3 songs each, things were going smoothly. Sometimes I was in the front and sometimes I'd allow others to take the lead, each of us trusting our assorted phone apps to lead the way.

Our 6th or 7th house was one of the unfamiliar ones. I'd added her to the list thinking she'd appreciate and enjoy a little merriment and, as far as I'd known, the group hadn't visited her in previous years. In fact, I'd never been to her house for a visit either, so it truly was the blind leading the blind.

Another car led the caravan to this particular street. We all climbed out of our vehicles and began searching for house numbers, which seemed poorly marked on many. Finally convinced we'd found the right place, someone knocked on the door and we broke into song as one from our group handed over a fruit basket to the first person to answer. In fact, the entire family came to listen with looks of joy and bewilderment on their faces, the one receiving the basket appearing especially perplexed at our presence.

And then it finally dawned on us that we were at the wrong house.

As this realization swept over the group, we pressed on with our singing as if the whole thing had been planned. Yes, of course we meant to stop here. And this lovely arrangement of produce is definitely for you and not someone else. We're glad to have finally met in person, whoever you are.

The house we actually wanted was right across the street. Luckily, we had more than one basket.

Nobody seemed all that upset that we'd made an extra stop. By the time we bade our new friends farewell we could already laugh about it. I still know nothing about the family we serenaded that night or whether the experience was at all enjoyable on their end, but as the reality of what was happening sank in halfway through "Joy to the World," we didn't really care.

We were out to share the season's spirit of love with people, and if that meant a few we hadn't meant to see, all the better. There's plenty to go around.

Fourth Wednesday of Advent: Moments

For several years now, my relationship with this season has been changing.

It's been quite a long time since I anticipated Christmas as being a magical winter wonderland where angels are always singing and everything is mint-flavored awesome. Many people I know operate with this view: this time brings them endless joy, and far be it for me to deny it to them or shame them for it. But for some reason, I don't experience that anticipation myself.

I certainly have my moments. I love the way my kids' eyes widen as they look at the decorations and listen to the story of the Polar Express. I still laugh at Clark's attempts to have the perfect holiday with his family, recite every line along with Dickens' A Christmas Carol, and become misty-eyed when Linus stands onstage to recite the passage from Luke. I look forward to carols on Christmas Eve and cinnamon rolls the next day. I savor the mornings before dawn when no one else is yet awake and I can drink my coffee by the light of the tree. There is plenty that I treasure about this time of year.

But mixed up in the magic is the mess. There's the memory of people who won't be joining us this year. There's the busyness of preparation that I inevitably get caught up in. There's the consumeristic barrage that makes me tired and the artificial cheer that companies constantly try to force upon us.

And so I daydream about sitting in a pub or I appreciate modest lighting displays on houses, and I think that there's something more real about that than the other stuff. There's something more true to the human experience where joy is truly able to break through despair rather than be slathered over top of it.

For some, December is one long continuous moment of wonder and glad tidings. Again, I don't deny them that and am happy that they can approach it that way. My own moments with family or favorite movies and songs come and go, and speak into a place of longing.

But I guess that's really what this time leading up to Christmas is about. We are searching and longing and waiting for something. When we finally find it, it's best to hold on. Because those other moments happen, too.

Fourth Thursday of Advent: Song

There come certain points in the day when it is very clear when my infant daughter was ready for a nap. It would take her a while longer to realize this for herself, and in those instances I had a few go-to tactics. The one that I used the most is walking around the house while rocking her and patting her back. It's not really a creative or unusual practice, but she liked the movement.

In those earliest months, I noticed that she seemed to be a big music fan. Whether the radio in the car, or Spotify just before bedtime, I discovered that music had a calming effect for her.

Oftentimes when I'd be rocking her during the day, it would come at a moment's notice and I don't have the hands available to cue something up on the computer or stereo. So I sang instead.

The song selection varies. I most often go to Five Iron Frenzy and Counting Crows (the latter worked really well with my son back in the day), but hymns seemed to work really well, too. And, with her youngest months coming close to December, it brought some inspiration to sing Christmas carols.

What I thought to be most appropriate when trying to rock an upset 3-month-old to sleep were those carols that are meant to be sung at a lower volume to begin with. What made this even more convenient is that several carols actually seem like lullabies, namely "Silent Night" and "Away in a Manger." As a pastor, I'd refuse to have the congregation sing these songs before Christmas Eve, but for the purposes of calming down an infant, they do just fine.

Now, let's be honest. These two carols are a bit silly. They make bold, inaccurate claims about a baby that doesn't cry and that has an extra special divine glow about him. He's a human baby. That's a big part of the whole incarnation thing. The cynical part of me scoffs at such lyrics. But when I sing these songs to a small child, who after a verse or two has calmed down and is even smiling up at me by this point, making those first exploratory language sorts of sounds, the innocence of the song connects with the fragile gentleness of the one I'm holding and it makes perfect sense.

I may return to that cynicism later on. But at least for a moment, those lyrics are true because I see the world's need for them.

Fourth Friday of Advent: Playlist

When it comes to Christmas music, I have become quite picky. This comes from years of radio stations and stores playing the same grouping of seasonal songs every year, without fail and without variation.

Even though my relationship with this time of year has improved, this lack of creativity in musical selection was one of the contributors to that relationship being a bit on the sour side. I don't need to hear "Rocking Around the Christmas Tree" and "Feliz Navidad" every day for two months straight. Even once a year is pushing it anymore.

So years ago, I opted to begin curating my own Spotify playlist for this time of year, having decided to be a bit more proactive about this annual annoyance. To help drive home the point, I even named it "Highly Superior Christmas Playlist."

Yes, I am that much of a snob about this.

The playlist has evolved over the years. The original had more punk and third wave ska on it, but songs have been removed and added as my preferences have slowly shifted. There are more acoustic and reflective tracks on it than there used to be. What began as an act of defiance has become more melancholy and meditative, which has kept in line with the mood that December has held for me.

Two songs on this list will likely never be removed. Even if I exchange every other song going forward, these two will likely remain. The first is "All I Ever Get for Christmas is Blue" by Over the Rhine. It describes spending the day in with a loved one while watching the snow fall and avoiding the holiday's commercialism. Plus I like to imagine listening to this song in the basement of a bar on like December 27th with nothing else to do but sip bourbon and feel my feelings, and believe it or not, I find that image comforting.

The second is "X'Mas Time (It Sure Doesn't Feel Like It)" by The Mighty Mighty Bosstones. It brings to mind similar imagery and feelings, and at the height of my yearly holiday funk, this was one of the perfect songs to name it.

Does it feel like Christmas time yet? Some of us may say ask again next year. Most of us may at least try a little harder to achieve "normal," even if that's been slow-going for several years. But there's only so much we can do by our own power, and holding our traditions loosely in the hope that something new might cause us pleasant surprise on its own might be our best course.

After all, Christmas is based on a strange and pleasant surprise. Surely those haven't stopped after the first one.

Fourth Saturday of Advent: Words

"Do you want the German words included again?" She asked this with some noticeable trepidation in her voice, giving away her slight hope that I would say no.

"Yes, absolutely I would. Thank you."

And with that, the church secretary was back in her office to format the Christmas Eve bulletin.

I grew up attending Christmas Eve services in a UCC church with a German Reformed heritage. When they settled here, many of these congregations originally held their entire worship in German until eventually they voted to begin incorporating English, if not switching to it entirely. But as a nod to its history, my church had a tradition to sing the first verse of "Silent Night" in English, and then again in German, before continuing with the rest of the song:

Stille Nacht! Heilige Nacht!
Alles schläft; einsam wacht
Nur das heilige Elternpaar.
Das im Stalle zu Bethlehem war,
Bei dem himmlischen Kind,
Bei dem himmlischen Kind.

As with many churches, the sanctuary lights would be turned off at this point, and the only light came from the candles that everyone held, the flame passed from one to another before joining in this beloved carol.

So I knew this tradition in my formative years. When I was called to pastor a church that didn't observe this I didn't think to add it, although in many of those years I travelled back to my hometown church to experience it during their late service. But once I began at a new church that had long observed it, I was resolved to keep it.

I may have earned a certain reputation as The Pastor Who Makes Us Do All These New Things over my years in local church ministry, but you can pull these German words on Christmas Eve from my cold, dead hands. Sure, that's overly dramatic, but church people are often overly dramatic when it comes to changing things, so I'll claim this one instance for myself.

If pressed to describe why I love hearing and singing these words during this moment so much, I suppose that my answer would be a sense of connection to a time and place in my past when this season only communicated beauty and truth and simplicity. For years and years, this day was only magical and warm and marked by reflective songs sung by candlelight.

This was before I lost loved ones we tended to see this time of year and before lean years when my wife and I couldn't afford to give each other very much. This was before visits to see one side of the family stopped with the death of my last grandparent. This was even before I had to start leading these services—with all the accompanying expectations—rather than getting to sit through them with everyone else.

Before all of that, there were these words, and so much else, and they helped make Christmas what it is.

And even despite all those changes and developments and losses, they still do.

So now I'm keeping them. Always.

Christmas Eve and Christmas Day

Christmas Eve: Interrupted

I wonder what it was like.

I wonder what it was like for Joseph, aspiring carpenter, engaged to Mary, setting up a nice little niche for himself in his corner of the world. Then he gets the news: Mary is pregnant. His life is interrupted. But God reassures him that all will be well.

I wonder what it was like for Mary, betrothed to Joseph, who is told she is with child through amazing means. What will Joseph say? How will she live in a world that frowns upon her situation regardless of the details? Her life is interrupted. But God reassures her that all will be well.

I wonder what it was like for the shepherds, working folk going about their nightly duties on a hillside when a chorus of angels, bright and booming, sing to them of something wondrous in the nearby city. Their lives are interrupted. But God reassures them that all will be well.

And I wonder what it was like for Zecharias, Elizabeth, Simeon, Anna, and the unnamed families and friends who undoubtedly were a part of this unfolding drama, who'd been used to certain ways that things just happen, until one day they don't happen like that anymore. One day they are given news that everything is going to be different.

Was it exciting? Or terrifying? Or did it produce untold anxiety? Were people stunned to the point of paralysis? Did some immediately launch into what they knew needed to be done in response? Did people allow themselves to grieve what was passing away, even if the future held possibility that they couldn't yet see?

We don't need to wonder what it was like, because we know. We've shared or received news like this: birth or death, marriage or divorce, illness or recovery, loss of a home or a new home to be made, a new job or retirement, hellos and goodbyes.

And somehow God was present in each one. God's good news has always been intertwined with the news of our lives. With change and loss comes new birth; possibilities we may not even be able to see. Regardless of our own ability to understand, divine forces sing us to the manger to see what newness awaits us.

Our lives are interrupted. But God reassures us that all will be well.

Christmas Day: Calm

I feel the busyness of this time of year just as many others do.

I have decorations to hang, gifts to buy, family activities to help prepare, and special church events to plan and lead.

At times, the weight of all of this causes my spirit to sag, and I want it all to be over with as quickly as possible. And then I start thinking about departed loved ones and commercialism and all the despair in the world that disrupts this season's joyful intentions. I grumble and grouse and I get angry at myself for feeling this way because I don't want to dampen the holiday experience for anyone else.

But at other times, I'm calm. I hear a favorite carol or laugh at a favorite movie or watch the candle flame flicker or the tree lights glow. I watch my congregation all gathered in one place pass the light to each other, and then I sip wine with my wife, the kids tucked in, and I drift to sleep gratefully anticipating the morning.

All is finally calm. All is finally bright. And I remember that I love Christmas still.

About the Author

Rev. Jeff Nelson serves as Minister for Ministerial Calls and Transitions as part of the national staff of the United Church of Christ. He is also a certified spiritual director in the Ignatian tradition. An active writer and blogger, his writing has appeared at New Sacred, the Christian Century blog, the Shalem Institute blog, The Englewood Review of Books, and The High Calling.

Read more at www.jeffreyanelson.com.